Waves Of Glory

Fiona Antoni

Scripture references taken from the New King James Version, Copyright © 1982 by Thomas Nelson, Inc.

Copyright © 2007 Fiona Antoni

All rights reserved. No part of this publication may be reproduced, stored in a retrieval system, or transmitted in any form or by any means, electronic, mechanical, photocopying, recording, or otherwise, without the prior written permission of the publisher.

ISBN: 978-1-60383-027-0

Published by:
Holy Fire Publishing
Unit 116
1525-D Old Trolley Rd.
Summerville, SC 29485

www.ChristianPublish.com

Cover Design: Jay Cookingham

Printed in the United States of America and the United Kingdom

Dedication

Dedicated to those who are;

- Living in a hopeless situation
- Broken-hearted
- Disappointed, having lost sight of their dreams
- Waking up each day in dread and fear
- Desperate to see a change in their lives
- Believing in a God of miracles yet not seeing any change in their situation?

I want you to know that your loving heavenly Father sees your tears and your pain and is not standing helplessly looking over you but is waiting for the appointed time for your miracle. He is not a cruel God but full of compassion and grace and if you will only trust in Him He will bring you though all your trials.

<u>DON'T GIVE UP !!!</u>

You are SPECIAL in the sight of God.

CONTENTS

Preface	7
Jesus My Everything	9
My Bridge Over Troubled Water	11
The Storms of Life	12
It May Be Today	15
His Ways Are Higher Than Your Ways	16
The Valleys May Be Low	19
Blessings through Pain	21
The Battle Belongs to the Lord	22
What a Saviour	25
Jesus Will Never Let You Down	27
Preparation Time	29
Listen to God's Word	31
Wait a Little Longer	33
His Appointed Time	35
When Heartache and Pain Is Your Lot	37
Amidst the Pain and Hardship	39
You Are My Everything	41

You Are Always There	43
Thank You Jesus	45
When Problems Overtake You	47
My Grace Is Sufficient	49
Don't Give Up	51
Run the Race	53
The Road May Be Dark	55
Cast All Your Cares on Him	57
Are You Feeling Discouraged?	59
Yet I Will Rejoice	61
Suddenly	63
Jesus Name Above All Names	65
Especially For You	66
You Are the Greatest	69
Jesus I Will Love You Forever	71
The Goodness of the Lord	73

Preface

For many years my life seemed like a battlefield with war on every side. The pain I felt as a result of my huge problems and difficulties was almost too hard to bear, despite having a very strong faith in the Lord.

In spite of my problems I learned how to worship and found that when I was engulfed in God's presence my problems seemed so much smaller, I drew closer to Him and would go to any meeting, where I knew I would sense "Waves of His Glory." Slowly I began to see improvements and my life started to change. Today I can only marvel at what God has done for me.

I started writing poems in 2000 and I often had tears rolling down my face as I wrote them. The Holy Spirit gave me words of encouragement and hope which enabled me to keep on going. Through the poems He promised me that I would come out of my difficulties and that He would use them for His glory. As I read these poems I would always feel encouraged and I soon began to realise that these poems were not just for me but for others in similar situations, so I compiled them into this book.

As you read these poems I pray that the Holy Spirit will minister to your heart and that whatever you are going through you will find your strength in Him. Remember He is a miracle working God and what you are going though today does not determine your tomorrow.

Whatever storm you are facing today is not too rough for the Lord to calm. Just trust in Him and worship Him and He will give you the ability to surf on the very waves that were sent to take you under.

God heard my cries and pleas and has done great things for me and I believe He will do the same for you.

JESUS
    My Saviour
    My King
    My Shepherd
    My Friend
    My Stronghold
    My Shield
    My Defence
    My Provider
    My Lord
    MY EVERYTHING

Whom have I in heaven
But You?
And there is none upon
Earth that I desire besides You.
My flesh and my heart fail;
But God
Is the strength of my heart
And my portion forever.

Psalm 73 verses 25 & 26

My Bridge over Troubled Water

You are my bridge over troubled water
My shelter from the storm
In sinking sand, You're my solid rock
Your arms forever safe and warm

You're my fortress when in danger
My help when I'm distressed
My lifeline when I'm drowning
In chaos You're my rest

You are my friend when I am lonely
You're my strength when I am weak
You lift me up when I am down
Your presence is all I seek

You lead me as a shepherd
You shine light upon my way
You are everything I need
What more can I say?

JESUS YOU ARE EVERYTHING TO ME

Then He arose and rebuked the wind and said to the sea "Peace be Still" and the wind ceased and there was a great calm.

Mark 4 verse 39

The Storms of Life

Though the sea may be deep
And the waves thrashing high
The thunder is crashing
Rain falls from the sky
You're far from the land
The boat rocks to and fro
The fear begins to rise
As the winds begin to blow
But don't worry at all
For the land is in sight
Just trust in your Master
He'll see you all right
For He is used to the waves
The storms, He can calm
When He's in the boat
There's no need for alarm
When it seems like Jesus
Is asleep in your boat
Don't worry He is with you
He will keep you afloat

For He knows where you are going
And you will reach the other side
He will never let you drown
Just in Him abide
For with Jesus in your boat
The storm will be stilled
The victory will be sweet
And with peace you'll be filled.

Be merciful to me,
O God,
Be merciful to me!
For my soul trusts in You;
And in the shadow of Your wings
I will make my refuge,
Until these calamities have passed by.

Psalm 57 verse 1

It May Be Today!

Your problems will not last forever
Very soon they will come to an end
For Jesus is your deliverer
He is your redeemer and friend

It doesn't matter how long you have suffered
It doesn't matter how long you have strived
For the Lord will bring your deliverance
At His appointed time

He waits till your faith has been tested
Till your faith in Him is secure
Will you trust Him enough to be patient?
Will you wait just a little while more?

You may feel tempted to give up
When hard times fall on your way
But be strong and be patient
Your breakthrough may happen today!

"For My thoughts are not your thoughts, nor are your ways My ways," says the Lord.. "For as the heavens are higher than the earth, so are My ways higher than your ways and My thoughts than your thoughts."
Isaiah 55 verses 8 & 9

His Ways Are Higher Than Your Ways

When you don't understand just what is going on
And problems are so hard to bear
Remember His ways are not your ways
It's not that He doesn't care
Because problems come and upset you
And you often ask the question," why?"
He answers "Just love Me and trust Me
I am God I cannot lie"
What He has promised is yours for the asking
And good things will come in their season
For the troubles you go through are helping you grow
And behind suffering there's always a reason
For He knows the end from the beginning
He knows what your future will hold
So don't question His wisdom or direction
He needs to refine you as gold
So when you are in the midst of trials
Don't complain about the problems you bear
Because His ways are higher than your ways
Just draw strength from Him in prayer

For when the trials are over
You will look back and understand
Just how the Lord sustained you
You'll see the touch of His hand
So trust Him this day with your situation
He will bring you through
And you will see His glory
And the blessings He has for you.

He gives power to the weak,
And to those who have no might,
He increases strength.
Even the youths shall faint and be weary,
And the young men shall utterly fall
But those who wait on the Lord
Shall renew their strength,
They shall mount up with wings like eagles
They shall run and not be weary,
They shall walk and not faint.

Isaiah 40 verses 29 -31

The Valleys May Be Low

The valleys may be low
The mountains very high
The road may be rocky
It may be hard just "getting by"

But Jesus walks with you
Every step of the way
He will give the strength you need
To get you through each day

So reach out to Jesus
Let him relieve your pain
He will give you rest and peace
And fill you with joy once again.

Fear not, for I am with you:
Be not dismayed,
For I am your God.
I will strengthen you,
Yes I will help you
I will uphold you with
My righteous right hand.

Isaiah 41 verse 10

Blessings Through Pain

Give your pain to the Lord
He knows what you are going through
He makes the crooked pathways straight
He knows just what to do
You'll have to walk through valleys
Of darkness and despair
But He will give you hope again
Lift your heart to Him in prayer
You'll have mountains in your life
That seem so very high
But He will give the strength you need
He will help you to "get by"
He hears your tender hearts cry
And your tears are never in vain
For He will bring an answer
Give you joy instead of pain.
For if you have no trials
And experience no pain
You will never know the blessings
And the treasures you have to gain.

You will not need to fight in this battle. "Position yourselves, stand still and
See the salvation of the Lord, who is with you, O Judah and Jerusalem,
Do not fear or be dismayed; Tomorrow go out against them, for the Lord is
with you."

2 Chronicles 20 verse 17

The Battle Belongs To The Lord

Stand still and trust your God
He will see you through
For every battle that you've had
He has fought for you
You need to do nothing
Just stand and trust the Lord
Because He has to honour
All that is in His Word
He promises you protection
He gives His angels charge of you
He will not leave you in the battle
But He will carry you through
If you did not have a battle
You might never understand
The glory of the Lord
And the power of His hand
So remember if you're struggling
And despair is your only friend
Don't give up on God
This is the beginning, not the end

For what you go through today
Is just a stepping-stone for tomorrow
So if you understand this
You will have no room for sorrow
So don't worry life will get better
The blessings are on their way
Because today does not determine tomorrow
Tomorrow's another new day.

Every valley shall be exalted
And every mountain
And hill brought low;
The crooked places
Shall be made straight
And the rough places smooth;

Isaiah 40 verse 4

What A Saviour

When your mountains are high
And your valleys are low
Your pathways are narrow
And the winds always blow
The storms come and rage
And the waves crash and roll
And the problems you have
Cause anguish of soul
Don't fear for Jesus, is with you
Every step of the way
He will give you strength
And help you through each day
For He will squash your mountains
And raise your valley's high
He will calm the storms
And cause the winds to die.
HALLELUJAH -WHAT A SAVIOUR

Remember the word to Your servant,
Upon which
You have caused me to hope,
This is my comfort
In my affliction,
For Your word has given me life.

Psalm 119 verses 49 & 50

Jesus Will Never Let You Down

When confusion comes upon you
And you seem to have lost your way
Tell it all to Jesus
Pour out your heart when you pray

For He is a mighty God
And there's nothing He can't do
And He will move heaven and earth
To get an answer just for you

Nothing is impossible
When you are trusting in the Lord
Lean not on your own understanding
But only on His Word

For He will bring to pass
The promises He has given you
If only you will trust Him
You'll see what He will do.

JESUS WILL NEVER LET YOU DOWN.

For You, O God have tested us;
You have refined us,
As silver is refined.
You brought us into the net;
You laid affliction on our backs,
You have caused men to ride
Over our heads;
We went through fire
And through water;
But You brought us out
To rich fulfilment.

Psalm 66 verses 10 – 12

Preparation Time

Why are you so troubled?
Why are you so sad?
Why do you look back
At the good times you once had?
Because the trials you go through
Are preparing you for tomorrow
For when they are all over
Joy will replace your sorrow
For life can be difficult
And the mountains seem too high
But don't you be despondent
From your problems you will not die
For you need to be refined
To do the work for Him
And without the fire you go through
Your dross would stay within
For the Lord is preparing
A special way for you
And if you will endure
He'll have a work for you to do.

As for God,
His way is perfect;
The word of the Lord is proven;
He is a shield to all who trust in Him.

2 Samuel 22 verse 31

Listen To God's Word

Don't listen to the words you hear
Do not become distressed
Just focus on the Lord
And He will give you rest

He sees your pain, He stores your tears
He knows what you are going through
He's always faithful, always there
He's always true to you

What other's say doesn't matter
Read God's Word it is true
And He will keep His promises
And fulfil His Word to you.

For the vision is yet for an appointed time;
But at the end it will speak,
And it will not lie.
Though it tarries, wait for it;
Because it will surely come,
It will not tarry.

Habakkuk 2 verse 3

Wait A Little Longer

Wait just a little while longer
Be patient and wait on the Lord
For your answer is surely coming
Trust in Him and in His Word

For He knows the trials you've been through
He knows the heartache and pain
For every trial that you go through
Will be followed by rich gain

There is a time for your breakthrough to happen
Appointed by God on His throne
So patiently wait for His timing
Don't try to go it alone

So don't give up your faith
He will see you through
And everything you've waited for
Will surely come to you.

For Sarah conceived and bore
Abraham a son in his old age,
At the set time
Of which God had spoken to him.

Genesis 21 verse 2

His Appointed Time

When life is difficult
And situations hard to bear
Remember nothing is too hard for the Lord
Take it to Him in prayer
He knows the trials you go through
He sees your every need
Just hold on tight to Him
And go where He may lead
He walks with you through valleys
And guides you when the light is dim
He will not leave you helpless
Just draw your strength from Him
Don't think that He has left you
When your situation stays the same
Just trust in Him completely
There is power in His name
When the appointed time has come
Just as Sarah had her son
You will have your breakthrough
The victory will be won
So don't lose heart and don't give up
Your break through is on the way
For when God appoints a time it happens
Maybe it will be today!!!!!.

He sent from above, He took me;
He drew me out of many waters,
He delivered me from my strong
enemy,
From those who hated me,
For they were too strong for me.
They confronted me in the day
Of my calamity,
But the Lord was my support:
He also brought me out into a broad
place;
He delivered me because
He delighted in me.

Psalm 18 verses 16 – 19

When Heartache and Pain Is Your Lot

When heartache and pain is your lot
And the answer seems so far away
Remember Jesus is at hand to help you
Just lift your voice and pray

Your suffering will not last your lifetime
And soon your deliverance will come
Jesus will help and guide you
Your victory has already been won

He longs to touch and bless us
But sometimes we shut Him away
For doubt and fear and worry
Hinder us so we don't pray

So lift up your heart to Jesus
Amidst the trouble and the strife
He will touch you and bless you
And bring changes into your life.

Though I walk in the midst of
trouble,
You will revive me;
You will stretch out Your hand
Against the wrath of my enemies,
And Your right hand will save me
The Lord will perfect
That which concerns me;
Your mercy, O Lord endures forever;
Do not forsake the works of Your
hands.

Psalm 138 verses 7 & 8

Amidst the Pain and Hardship

Amidst the pain and hardship
Jesus is there for you
He will help and guide you
He will see you through

Your troubles may be large
Your situation too hard to bear
But Jesus is your refuge
Just trust in His loving care

When you cry He always answers
So do not be distressed
Just trust in Him completely
And He will give you rest

For the problems you are going through
Are definitely not here to stay
For at any moment they can change
Your miracle may happen today.

The Lord is my strength
And my shield;
My heart trusted in Him,
And I am helped;
Therefore my heart greatly rejoices,
And with my song
I will praise Him.

Psalm 28 verse 7

You Are My Everything

You are my everything
You are my all
 Without You in my life
I would surely fall
You are my "Rock of Ages"
My Deliverer my Friend
The Alpha, Omega
The Beginning the End
With You in my life
I can weather the storm
Whatever the shape
Whatever the form
The mountains are flattened
The valleys raised high
I know in the wilderness
I will not die
You are so faithful
So kind and so true
My life would be empty
If it wasn't for You
Jesus my Saviour
My Redeemer My King
With my whole heart to You
Praises I'll sing.

Where can I go from your Spirit?
Or where can I flee from Your presence?
If I ascend to heaven. You are there
If I make my bed in hell, behold You are there
If I take the wings of the morning,
And dwell in the uttermost parts of the Sea,
Even there shall Your hand shall lead me,
And Your right hand shall hold me.

Psalm 139 verses 7 - 10

You Are Always There

When my life is in turmoil
You're always there
In the dark of the night
You're always there
When friends despise me
You're always there
When I feel lonely
You're always there
In depression, in rejection
You're always there
When I don't feel your presence
You're always there
How do I know?
Because You said
"I will <u>NEVER</u> leave you nor forsake you"

"Fear not, for I have redeemed you;
I have called you by your name:
You are Mine.
When you pass through the waters,
I will be with you;
And through the rivers,
They shall not overflow you.
When you walk through the fire,
You shall not be burned,
Nor shall the flame scorch you.
For I am the Lord your God,
The Holy One of Israel,
Your Saviour."

Isaiah 43 verses 1 – 3

Thank You Jesus

Thank you Jesus
That You are always with me
Though the fire may be hot
I will not be burned
Though the flames may lick me
I will not be scorched
Though the waters may be deep
I will not drown
Though the mountains may be high
I will climb them
Though the valleys may be low
I will come out of them
Though my enemies may rise against me
I will not be overtaken
Though my afflictions may be many
I will be delivered of them all
Thank you Jesus
That whatever I go through
Cannot be too much for me
IF YOU ARE BY MY SIDE.

Blessed is the man
Who endures temptation;
For when he has been approved,
He will receive the crown of life
Which the Lord had promised
To those who love Him.

James 1 verse 12

When Problems Overtake You

When problems overtake you
And obstacles block your way
Don't worry Jesus will help you
Your problems are not here to stay

The going may be tough
And the pain too hard to bear
But it will not last forever
Just abide in His loving care

He hates to see us suffer
And it grieves Him when we're in pain
But He knows as we endure
We have so much to gain

For when we go through trials
Our faith becomes so strong
And we learn to trust our Master
Though the days may be hard and long

For when we have endured
We have a lot to gain
And joy and peace and happiness
Shall replace our pain.

Concerning this thing,
I pleaded with the Lord
Three times that it might
Depart from me.
And He said to me
"My grace is sufficient for you,
For My strength
Is made perfect in weakness."

2 Corinthians 12 verses 8 & 9

My Grace Is Sufficient

Lord I cannot bear this pain
Don't You know it's too much for me?
How can I take all this pain and survive?
"MY GRACE IS SUFFICIENT FOR YOU"

Don't You know my heart is breaking?
My tears are forever falling?
Why don't You stop this heartache?
"MY GRACE IS SUFFICIENT FOR YOU"

How can you stand to watch what happens?
Does it hurt You too?
When is it going to come to an end?
"MY GRACE IS SUFFICIENT FOR YOU"

Lord I chose this path
With its mountains and valleys
With trouble, hardship and pain
But now I know Lord
YOUR GRACE IS SUFFICIENT FOR ME

You number my wanderings
Put my tears into Your bottle
Are they not in Your book?
When I cry out to You.
Then my enemies will turn back;
This I know because God is for me,

Psalm 56 verses 8 & 9

Don't Give Up

Don't give up when troubles overtake you
When there are problems everywhere
Because your God in heaven
Will answer every prayer

He hears your weary voices
He stores your every tear
With Him nothing is forgotten
So you have no need to fear

For every trial is for your good
He never makes mistakes
Your burden is not too hard to bear
For He gives the strength it takes

Your tears will not be forever
And they will never be in vain
For joy comes in the morning
Just as sunshine after the rain

Remember your Father in heaven
Wants to bless you through and through
And when your trials are over
He'll have a work for you to do

Therefore do not cast away
Your confidence,
Which has a great reward.
For you have need of endurance,
So that after you have done the will
of God,
You may receive the promise:

Hebrews 10 verses 35 & 36

Run The Race

Run the race with vigour
Don't let your problems drag you down
For when the prize is given
You will receive your crown

The walk is seldom easy
But there is help along the way
Jesus is your strength and guide
To see you through each day

So endure the pain and hardship
And with patience run the race
And you will see His glory
And the riches of His grace.

For His anger is for a moment
His favour is for life
Weeping may endure for a night
But joy comes in the morning.

Psalm 30 verse 5

The Road May Be Dark

The road ahead may seem so dark
But Jesus will guide you through
He is the light in your darkness
He has a plan for you
Just take one day at a time
And hold fast to His strong hand
For when the pathway is uncertain
You have to understand
That he can see the path ahead
The way for Him is clear
Just trust in Him completely
And you will have no need to fear
For darkest nights always come to an end
And light comes as day is dawning
For sorrow may endure the night
But joy comes in the morning.

Cast your burden on the Lord,
And He shall sustain you;
He shall never permit
The righteous to be moved.

Psalm 55 verse 22

Cast All Your Cares on Him

Cast all your cares on Jesus
For He cares for you
Only on Him can you depend
He will carry you through

He listens to your hearts cry
He sees your every tear
He wants to take your burdens
And release you from all fear

The reason why we worry
And our hope begins to dim
Is because we keep our burdens
Instead of giving them to Him.

Oh how great is Your goodness,
Which You have laid up
For those who fear You,
Which You have prepared
For those who trust in You
In the presence of the sons of men!

Psalm 31 verse 19

Are You Feeling Discouraged?

Are you feeling discouraged?
Are your problems too hard to bear?
Don't give up on Jesus
He hears your every prayer
The answer may be long in coming
And clouds of despair follow you
But Jesus will keep His promises
Don't let doubt rob you of your view
For everything He has promised
Will surely come to pass
If only you will trust Him
You'll receive what you have asked.

Though the fig tree may not blossom,
Nor fruit be on the vine;
Though the labour of the olive may fail,
And the fields yield no food;
Though the flock may be cut off
From the fold,
And there be no herd in the stalls –
YET
I will rejoice in the Lord,
I will joy in the God of my salvation.
The Lord God is my strength;
He will make my feet like deer's feet,
and
He will make me walk on my high hills.

Habakkuk 3 verses 17 – 19

Yet I will Rejoice

Though the car may fail to start
And the roof is leaking
Though the job has finished
And there is no food in the house
Though my shoes have worn out
And my clothes have holes in them -

YET I will rejoice in the Lord,
I will joy in the God of my salvation.
The Lord God is my strength.
He will make me walk on my high hills

Though the debts are piling high
And the bills cannot be paid.
Though my children go astray
And my spouse hates me
Though my family desert me
And my friends forsake me -

YET I will rejoice in the Lord.
I will joy in the God of my salvation.
The Lord God is my strength.
He will make me walk on my high hills

And SUDDENLY a woman who had a flow of blood for twelve years came from behind and touched the hem of His garment ,For she said to herself, "If only I may touch His garment , I shall be made well." But Jesus turned and when He saw her He said," Be of good cheer daughter, your faith has made you well." And the woman was made well from that hour.

    Matthew 9 verses 20 - 22

Suddenly

Suddenly
The sick are healed
The blind see
The lame walk
The oppressed go free

Suddenly
The baby is conceived
The breakthrough comes
The prayer is answered
The enemy flees

Suddenly
Your spouse loves you
Your children are saved
Your needs are met
Your debts are paid

Suddenly
When the waiting seems forever
When fear and doubts flood in
When the darkness is at its worst

SUDDENLY
    God moves in His Power,
        Just as He promised!!!!

Therefore God also
Has highly exalted Him
And given Him the name
Which is above every name.
That at the name of Jesus
Every knee should bow,
Of those in heaven,
And of those on earth,
And of those under the earth,

Philippians 2 verses 9 & 10

Jesus Name Above All Names

Jesus name above all names
The name above every mountain in my life
The name above every disease
The name above every shame
Jesus name above all names

Jesus name above all names
The name above every debt
The name above every lack
The name above every need
Jesus name above all names

Jesus name above all names
The name above barrenness
The name above singleness
The name above unhappiness
JESUS THE NAME ABOVE EVERY OTHER NAME.

Especially For You

When you feel that all is lost
And you are broken through and through
When the tears begin to fall
And you don't know what to do
When you've lost the peace you had
And life has gone so wrong
It is time to look to Jesus
Come before him with a song
For there is power in your praises
And you will have the victory
For as you dance and sing
The Lord will set you free
For the precious Holy Spirit
Wants to heal you of your pain
To give you back your peace
And to free you from all shame
For nothing is too hard for Him
And no mistake too great
For He is a God of tenderness
He will correct but not berate
So whatever you have been through
Don't let it bring despair
Just learn from each experience
And get close to Him in prayer

For every thing you've been through
Makes your life seem such a mess
But God will use it for His glory
And through it He will bless
For when you are refined
And He has finished His work in you
Then He will give you the special job
That was designed ……………..ESPECIALLY FOR YOU

For who is God except the Lord?
And who is a rock except our God?
It is God who arms me with strength
And makes my way perfect
He makes my feet like the feet
Of deer's
And sets me on my high places.

Psalm 18 verses 31 – 33

You Are The Greatest

What a mighty God You are
So awesome so faithful and true.
You are my rock and my fortress
No one can compare with You

You are the Lily in my valley
The Light in my darkest hour
My Healer when I'm sick
When in danger my Strong Tower.

When others accuse you defend me
You lift me when I fall
My best friend when I'm lonely
My Saviour when I call

I can find no words to describe You
You are merciful and kind
On earth and in heaven
No one greater could I find.

I will love You, O Lord my strength
The Lord is my rock and my fortress
And my deliverer;
My God, my strength, in whom
I will trust;
My shield and the horn of my
salvation,
My stronghold.
I will call upon the Lord,
Who is worthy to be praised;
So shall I be saved from my enemies.

Psalm 18 verses 1- 3

Jesus I Will Love You Forever

Jesus I love You more than words can say
I will love You forever whatever may come my way
You are the light in my darkness
You are the joy in my heart
How I long for the day
When we will never part

Jesus I love You more than words can say
I will love You forever, whatever may come my way
You are the strength in my weakness
You are the comfort in my pain
You are the King of my life
And in my heart You will reign

Jesus I love You more than words can say
I will love You forever whatever may come my way
You are my refuge when I'm in trouble
You are my peace in the storm
Sheltering in Your arms
I feel so safe and warm

Jesus I love You more than words can say
I will love You forever whatever may come my way
You are my Lord, my brother
My husband, my friend
My future my past
The beginning and end.

I would have lost heart,
Unless I had believed
That I would see
The goodness of the Lord
In the land of the living.

Psalm 27 verse 13

The Goodness of the Lord

When my mind was in turmoil
And the pressures of life
Too much to handle
Full of trouble and strife
I would have lost heart
Had I not truly believed
That all that I'd prayed for
I would surely receive
For after the storms
Came a life full of blessing
And I saw the Lord's goodness
In the land of the living.

Lightning Source UK Ltd.
Milton Keynes UK
17 November 2009

146320UK00001B/64/A